Cora The Highland Cow
& The Day The Puppies Escaped

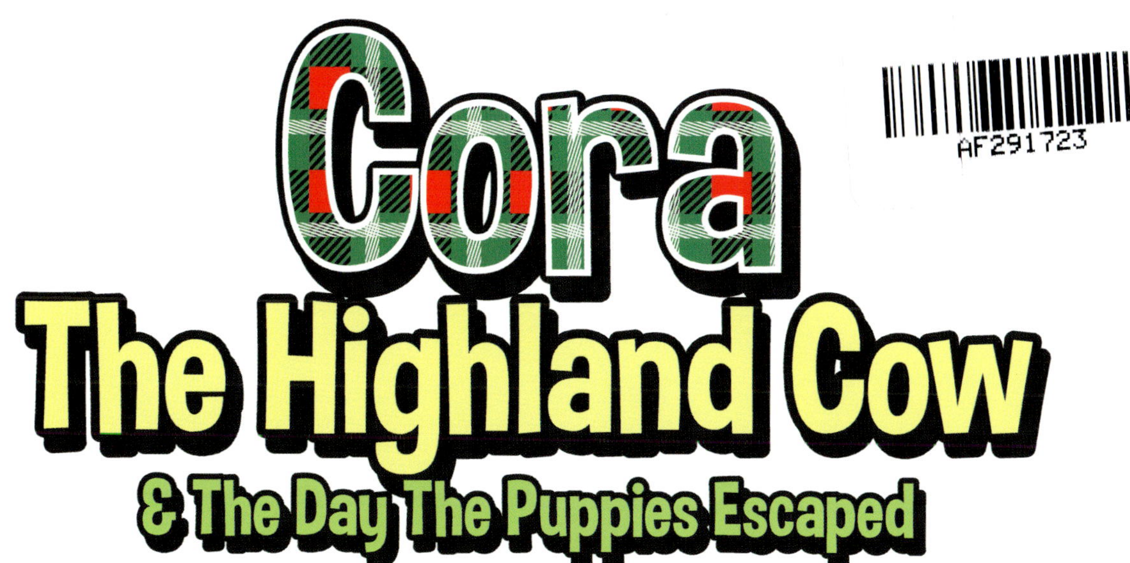

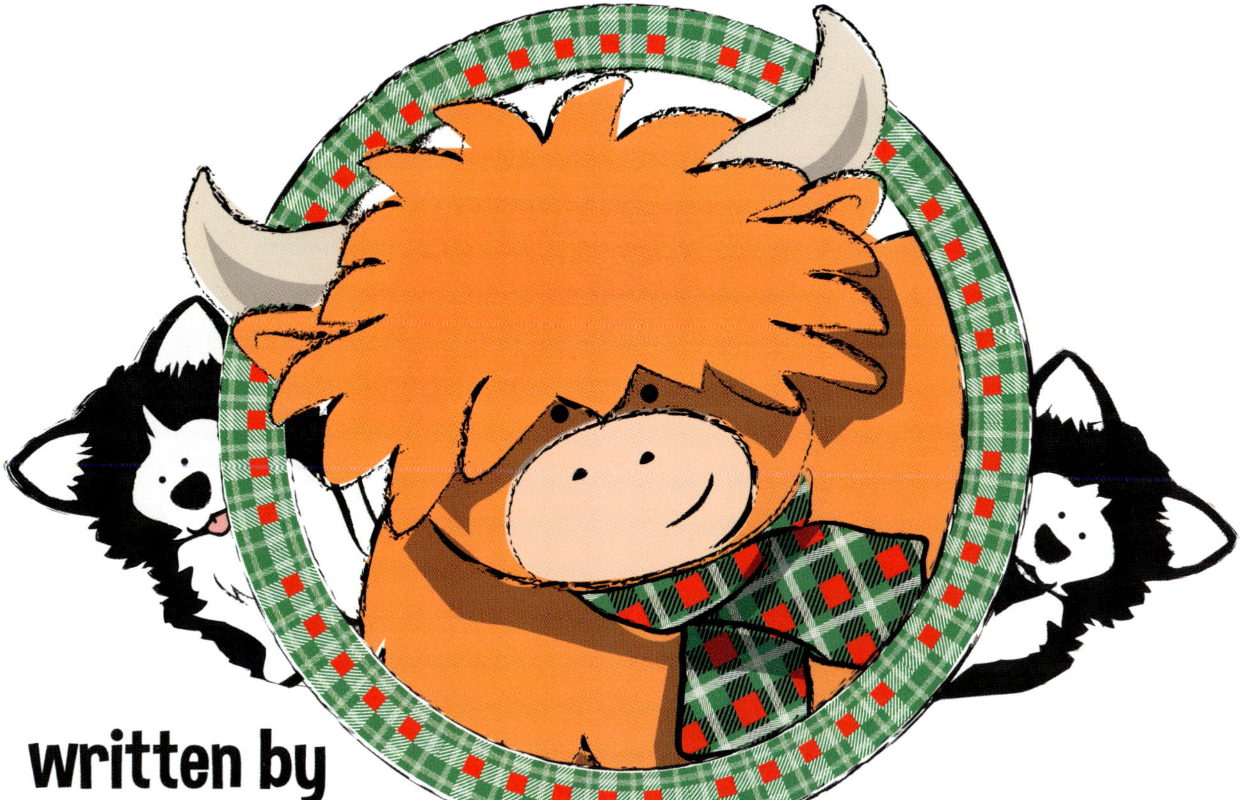

written by
Lizzie Wallace

illustrated by **BazMac**

Cora was a highland cow
who lived down on the farm,
You can find her and her farmyard friends
in the warm and cosy barn.

So today our story to be told,
made Cora want to shout,
when looking after sheepdog pups,
the day that they got out.

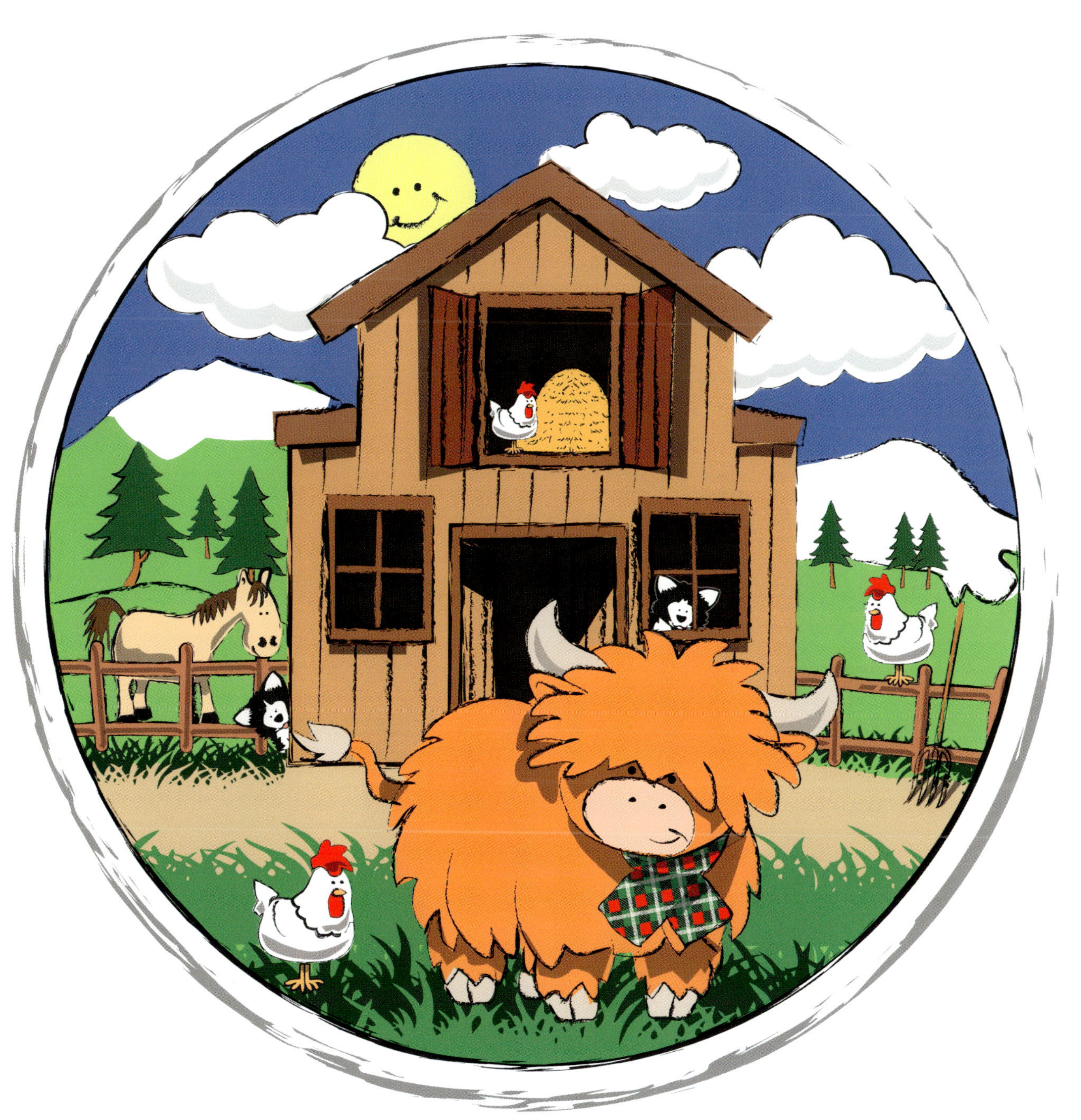

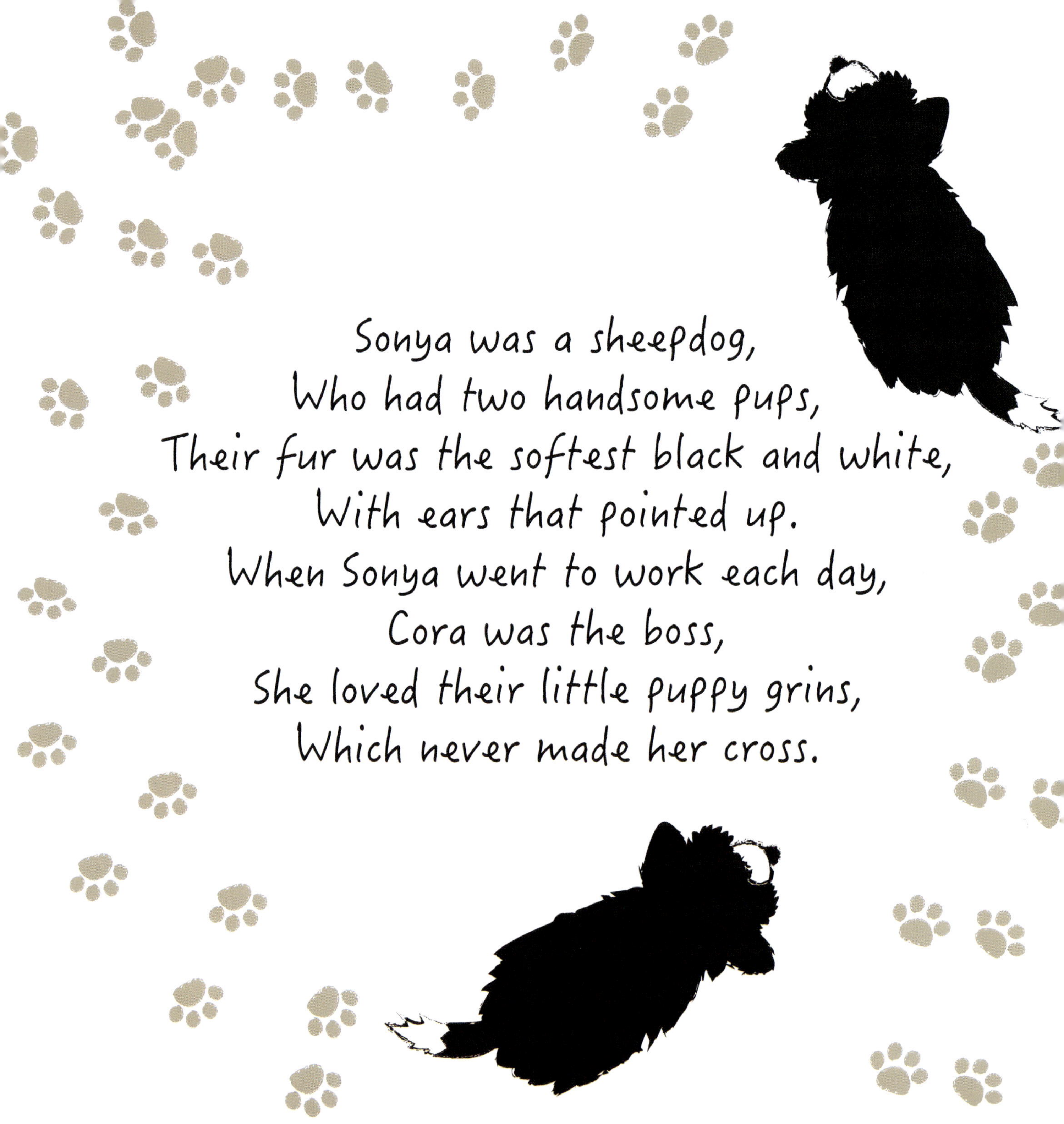

Sonya was a sheepdog,
Who had two handsome pups,
Their fur was the softest black and white,
With ears that pointed up.
When Sonya went to work each day,
Cora was the boss,
She loved their little puppy grins,
Which never made her cross.

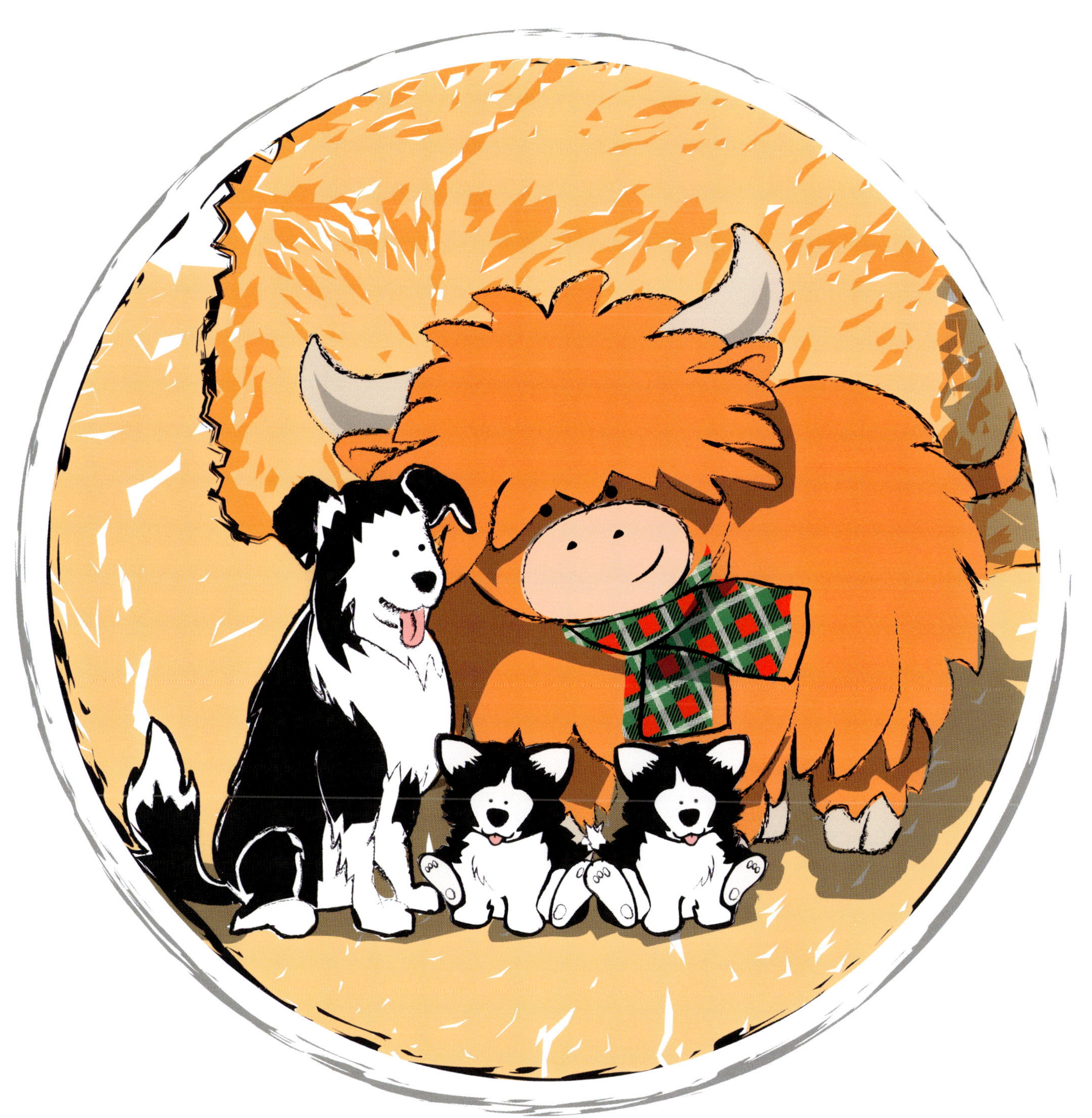

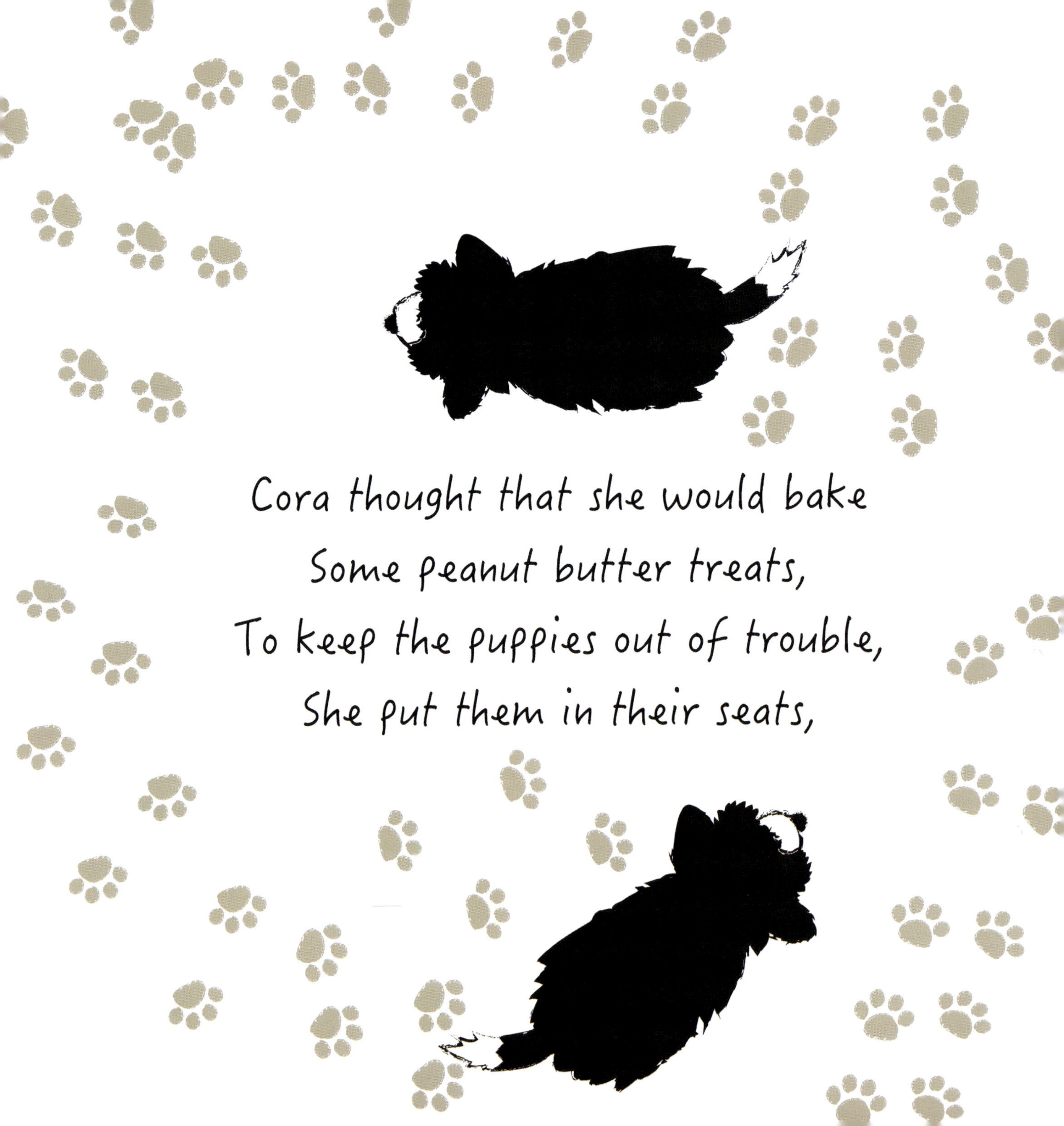

Cora thought that she would bake
Some peanut butter treats,
To keep the puppies out of trouble,
She put them in their seats,

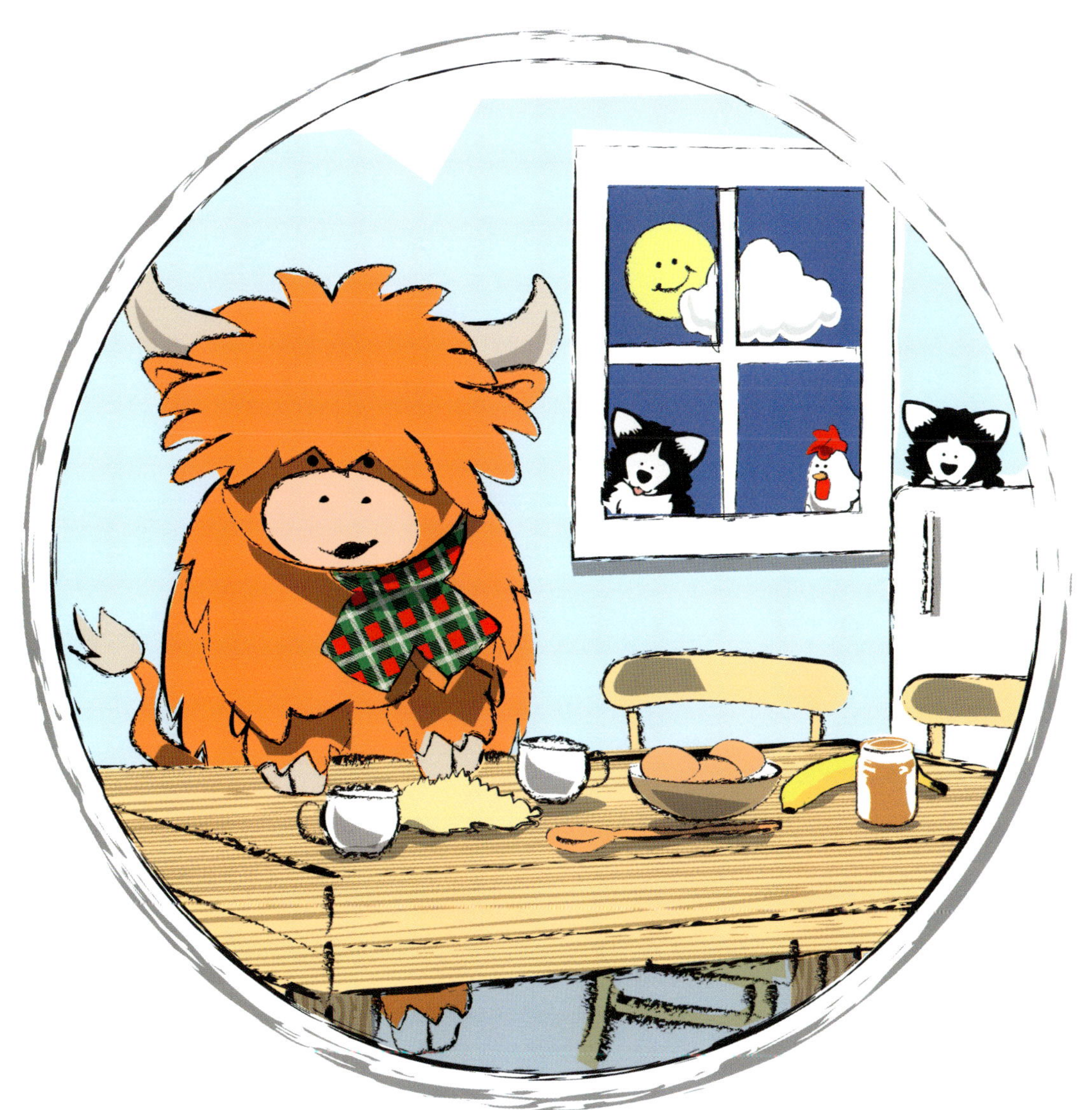

But unknown to Cora on that day,
The pups had learned a trick,
They wriggled when her back was turned
And escaped with a lick and a flick.

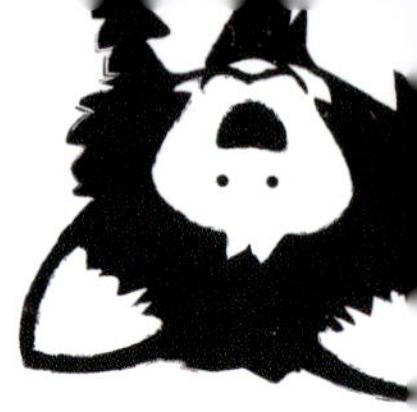

The pups snuck out the kitchen door, when
Cora turned around,
"Oh help, Oh Noooo" she mooed and squealed
"Where can the pups be found?"

She hunted cupboards high and low
And even in the loo,
There were no puppies to be found
What was a cow to do?

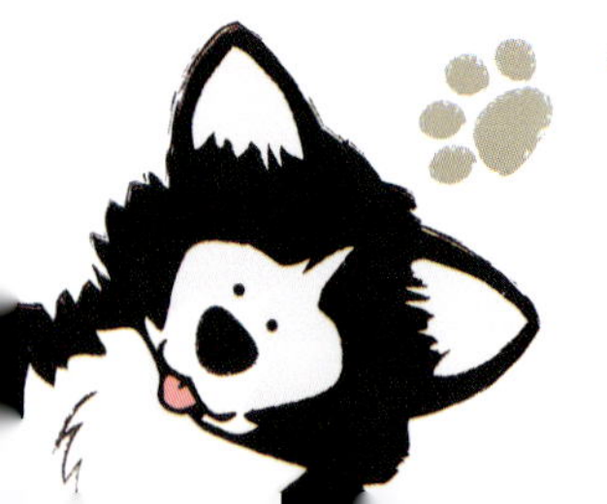
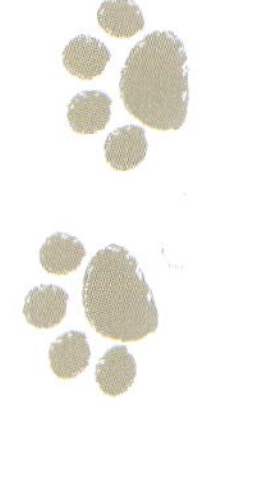

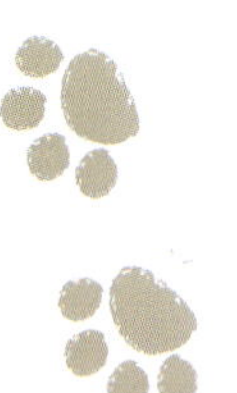

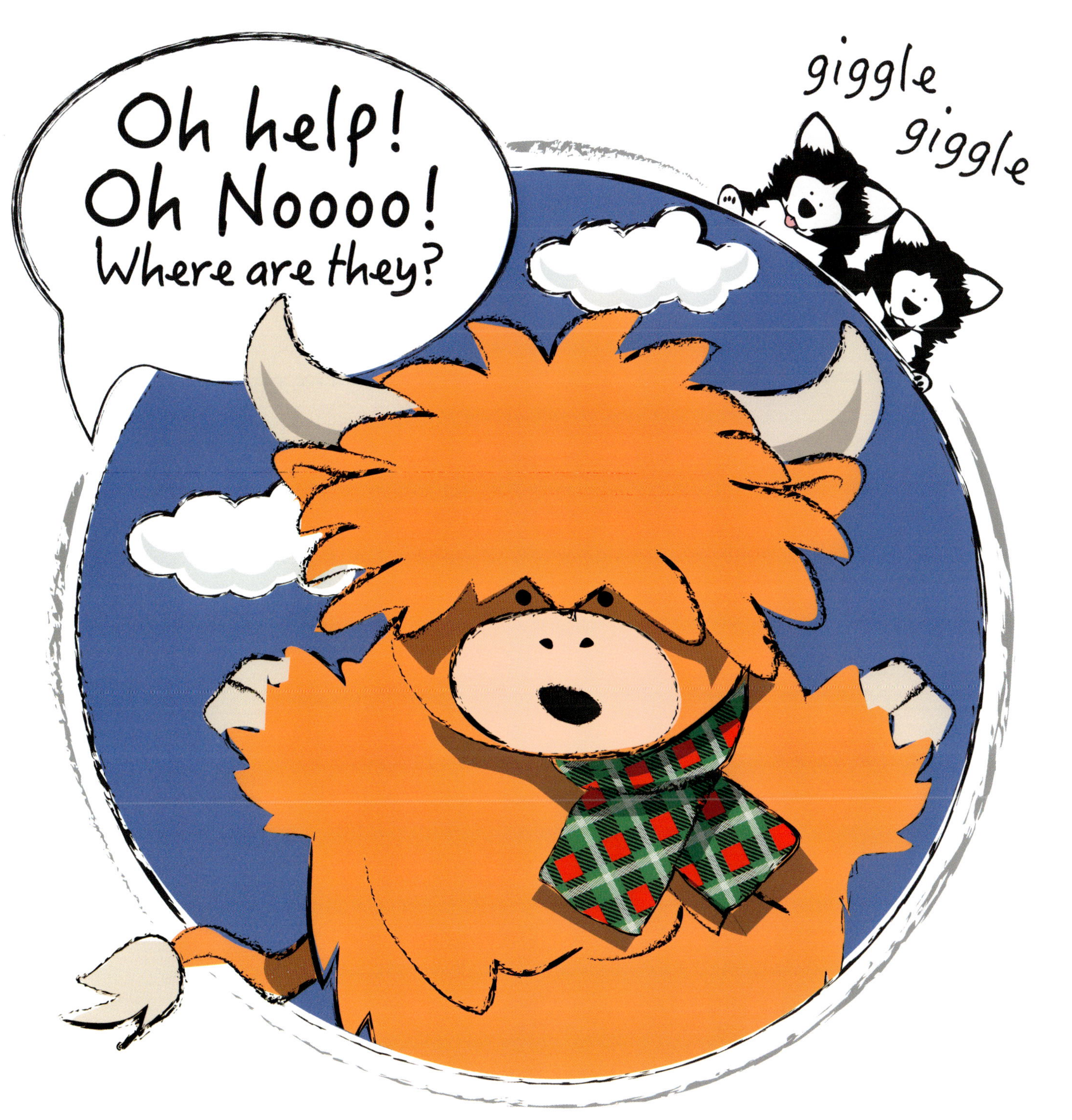

Oh help!
Oh Noooo!
Where are they?
giggle
giggle

She decided she would lay a trail
Of treats and yummy snacks
The pups would surely smell the food
And make their way right back.

Cora laid the biscuits down
On the path towards the barn,
There were many places pups could hide,
On a large and busy farm.

She hoped that the delicious smell
Would tempt the pups to come,
And sure enough soon puppy mouths were
Scooping up the crumbs.

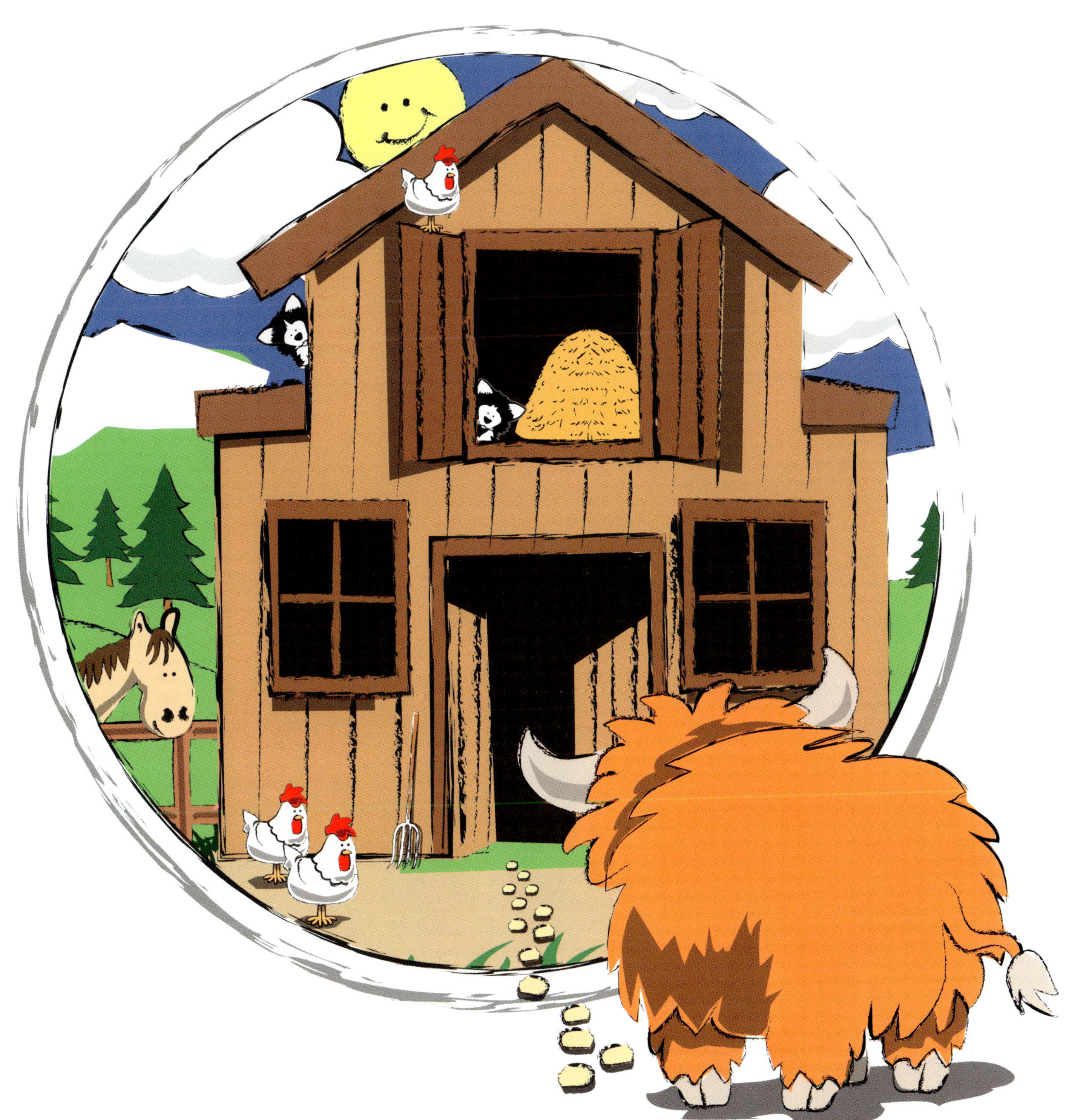

"I've found you" she mooed and
scooped them up Cora smiled with glee
"and just in time before your mum,
gets home to have her tea"

The puppies gave their cheeky grins
and settled down in the hay,
Tomorrow would bring more fun and games,
but today was a wonderful day!!

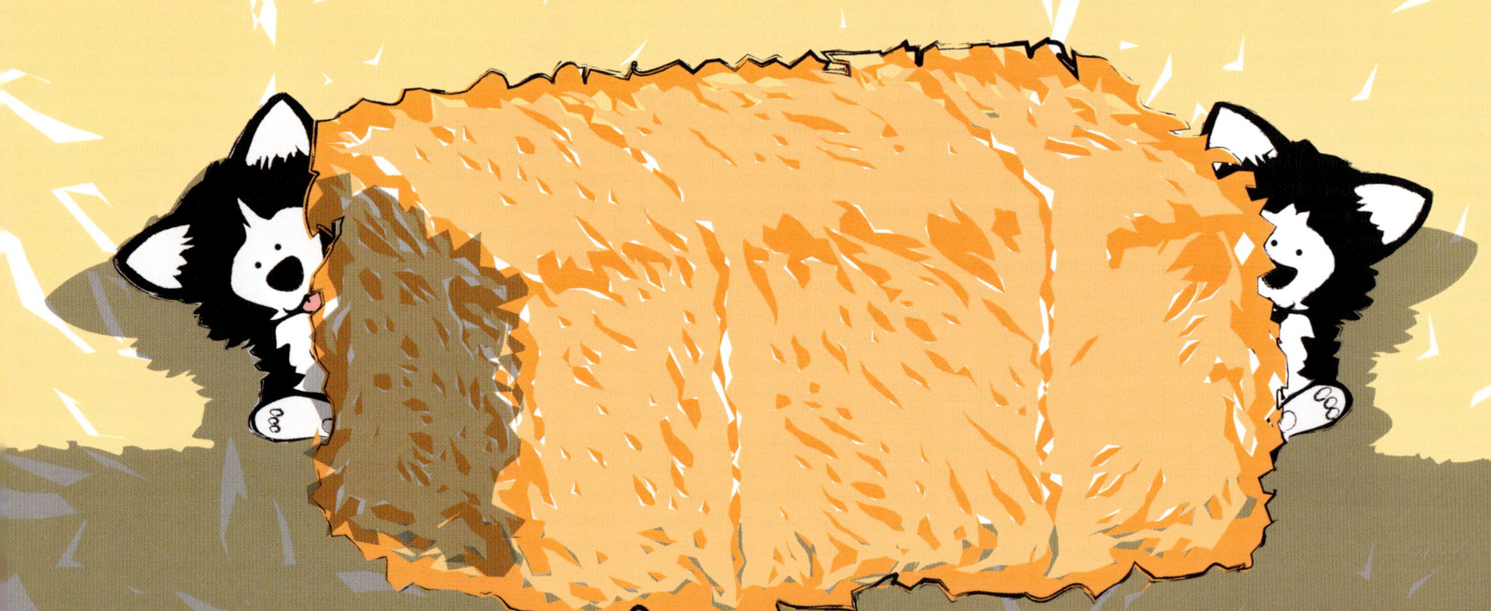

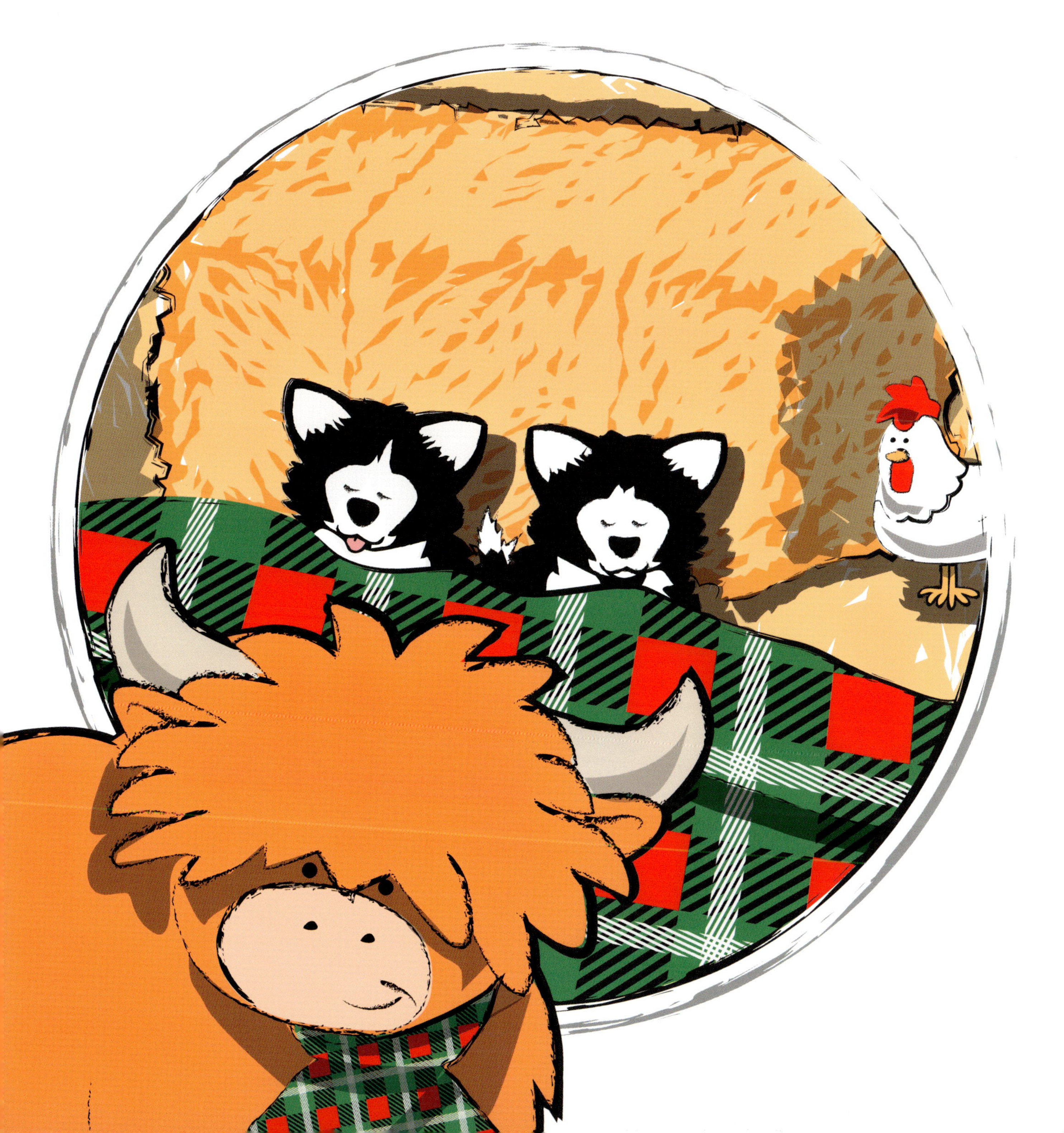

Recipe for doggy treats:

1 banana peeled, 1 cup oat flour
2/3 cup rolled oats, ½ cup dried parsley
3 tablespoons peanut butter, 1 egg beaten

Method

1. Preheat oven to 300F. Mash banana and then add oat flour, oats, parsley, peanut butter and egg. Mix well, set aside for 5 minutes.

2. Roll mixture into small dog sized treats. Transfer to lined baking tray and bake until firm and golden brown on the bottom, 40-45 minutes. Set aside to cool completely.

3. Store treats in air tight container at room temperature.

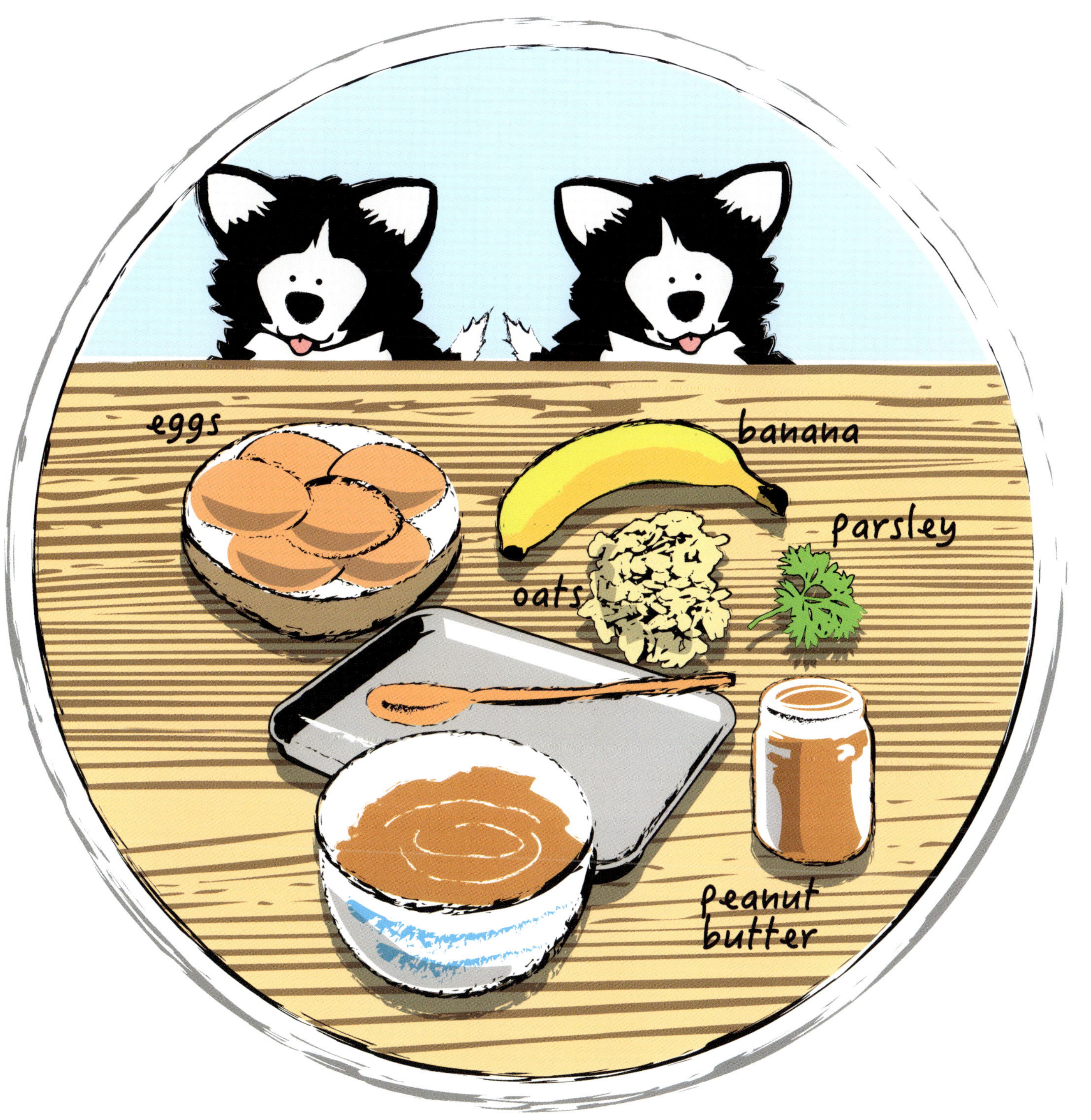

eggs
banana
parsley
oats
peanut
butter

Published by
i2i Publishing. Manchester.
http://www.i2ipublishing.co.uk

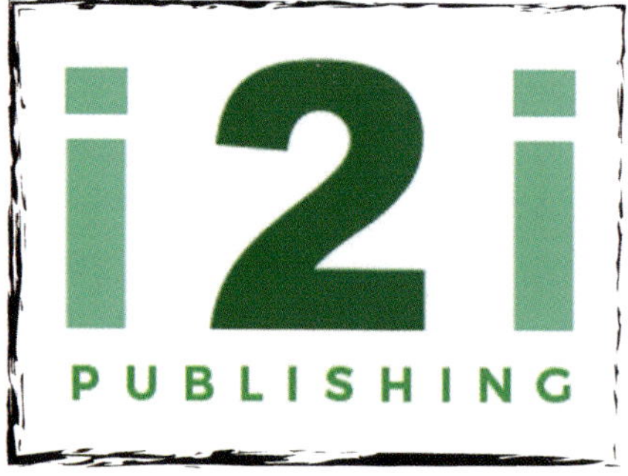